The Declaration of Independence and the Continental Congress

Matthew Betti

NEW YORK

Published in 2016 by The Rosen Publishing Group, Inc.
29 East 21st Street, New York, NY 10010

Library of Congress Cataloging-in-Publication Data

Betti, Matthew.
The Declaration of Independence and the Continental Congress / Matthew Betti. -- First Edition.
    pages cm. -- (Spotlight on American history)
Includes bibliographical references and index.
ISBN 978-1-4994-1731-9 (library bound) -- ISBN 978-1-4994-1728-9 (pbk.) -- ISBN 978-1-4994-1729-6
(6-pack)
1. United States. Declaration of Independence--Juvenile literature. 2. United States. Continental Congress--
Juvenile literature. 3. United States--Politics and government--1775-1783--Juvenile literature. I. Title.
E221.B53 2016
973.3'13--dc23
                                        2015018596

Manufactured in the United States of America

CPSIA Compliance Information: Batch #WS15PK: For Further Information contact Rosen Publishing, New York, New York at 1-800-237-9932

CONTENTS

JAN 3 2017

THE DOCUMENT THAT DECLARED INDEPENDENCE

On July 4, Americans celebrate Independence Day. Americans celebrate Independence Day in many ways. Some people hang flags on their homes. Some watch fireworks displays. Others dress up and march in parades.

On this day, in 1776, the American **colonies** adopted the Declaration of Independence. This **document** was an official announcement by the colonies. It said that they would no longer be ruled by Great Britain.

The Declaration of Independence was important. It stated the reasons why the people of the colonies believed they had the right to be free from British rule. It also argued that people had a right to choose their own government. The ideas in the Declaration of Independence are the same ideas on which the United States would be founded. The term "Declaration of Independence" was not used in the document. The document does, however, announce that the 13 colonies regarded themselves as the United States of America.

This actor is dressed in colonial clothing. He reads the Declaration of Independence outside the National Archives in Washington, D.C., on July 4.

GREAT BRITAIN AND THE 13 COLONIES

The relationship between Great Britain and the 13 colonies became strained after the **French and Indian War** ended in 1763. This was a war with France over the control of North America. Britain's **Parliament** passed new **taxes** to help pay for the war.

These taxes were unpopular with the colonists. Colonists were also unhappy that they had no **representatives** in Parliament to speak up about laws

This painting shows a battle scene in 1755 from the French and Indian War. In this conflict between the British and the French, each side was helped by colonists and Native Americans.

A political cartoon from 1767 shows the authors of the Stamp Act carrying the repealed law to its grave.

and taxes that affected them. They thought of themselves as British subjects, with the right to have representatives in Parliament. They thought it unjust to have taxation without representation.

The colonists **protested** the new laws and taxes passed by Parliament. These disagreements would lead to the **American Revolution**.

THE REVOLUTIONARY WAR BEGINS

In 1774, representatives from 12 of the 13 colonies met in Philadelphia, Pennsylvania. The group is now known as the First Continental Congress. Its members discussed how the colonies should respond to the Coercive Acts. These were laws that punished the colonies for protesting Parliament's laws and taxes. The American patriots called the laws the Intolerable Acts. They were passed by the British Parliament in 1774 after the Boston Tea Party.

The tensions between Great Britain and the colonies turned to war on April 19, 1775. On that day, colonists successfully fought British troops at the Battles of Lexington and Concord in Massachusetts. Though people sometimes think the Declaration of Independence started the war, more than a year would pass before this document was written!

The engraving shown here from 1872 celebrates the beginning of the American Revolution. The illustration shows the Battles of Lexington and Concord on April 19, 1775.

THE SECOND CONTINENTAL CONGRESS

Representatives from each of the colonies met again starting in 1775 at the Second Continental Congress to discuss the war effort. They set up an army, called the Continental army. They put the army under the command of George Washington.

Many people in the congress hoped to avoid a bigger war with Great Britain. Many wanted to remain part of the British colonies. In July, congress sent a letter to Britain's king, George III, asking for a peaceful solution. The king rejected this letter in August.

As the fighting continued into the next spring, congress met again to discuss whether a break from Britain was necessary. Many wanted to find a way to avoid this break. The language of a 1773 letter by Thomas Jefferson describes the conflict American colonists felt: "There is not in the British Empire a man who more cordially loves a union with Great Britain than I do. But by the God that made me, I will cease to exist before I yield a connection on such terms as the British parliament proposes."

Shown here are the leaders of the Continental Congress in 1775: John Adams, Robert Morris, Alexander Hamilton, and Thomas Jefferson. This illustration was made in 1894.

PATRIOTS AND LOYALISTS

At the start of the American Revolution, most colonists did not want independence from Britain. Colonial support for independence grew as the war went on. Colonists who were for independence were called patriots. Those who were not were called loyalists. Historians estimate that as many as 20 percent of the colonists remained loyalists throughout the war.

In this 1776 engraving, a loyalist is about to be tarred and feathered by his patriot neighbors during the American Revolution.

This engraving shows British and Hessian soldiers parading through New York City during the American Revolution. New York City was occupied for seven years.

Not every representative in the Second Continental Congress had permission from his colony's government to declare independence. However, by May 1776, the governments of eight colonies had voted for independence. The governments of Delaware, Maryland, New Jersey, New York, and Pennsylvania were holding back on declaring independence.

THE LEE RESOLUTION

On June 7, 1776, Richard Henry Lee of Virginia presented a **resolution** to the Second Continental Congress. It said the colonies were "free and independent states."

Voting on the Lee Resolution was put off until July 2. This was because the congress was still waiting for support for independence from the five remaining colonies. In the meantime, the congress chose Thomas

This is a portrait of Richard Henry Lee (1732-1794). Lee was a member of the Continental Congress and a signer of the Declaration of Independence.

The illustration shown here imagines the drafting of the Declaration of Independence in 1776. From left to right are Benjamin Franklin, Thomas Jefferson, John Adams, Robert Livingston, and Roger Sherman.

Jefferson to write a formal statement based on the Lee Resolution. Jefferson was aided by John Adams, Benjamin Franklin, Robert Livingston, and Roger Sherman to write this statement. It would list the reasons why the colonies were breaking away from Britain. It would become known as the Declaration of Independence.

LIFE, LIBERTY, AND THE PURSUIT OF HAPPINESS

The Declaration of Independence says that the colonies need to declare independence. It also says that they have the natural right to do this.

It outlines the colonists' beliefs that "all men are created equal" and have the right to "life, liberty, and the pursuit of happiness." It says that governments are formed or revolted against to protect these rights. Then

The William J. Stone engraving of the United States Declaration of Independence is the most frequently reproduced version of the document. It was created in 1823.

This illustration helps us imagine what Thomas Jefferson looked like when he was writing the Declaration of Independence.

it lists the colonists' complaints, such as being taxed without Parliamentary representation. It finishes by saying that, because these complaints have been ignored, the colonies are ending their ties to Britain and declaring themselves "free and independent states." These core concepts formed the philosophy of the new country.

JULY 4, 1776

The Declaration of Independence as we know it came together over a period of time. On June 28, 1776, Thomas Jefferson presented the draft that he and the four other representatives had written for the Second Continental Congress. Congress spent the next week discussing and making changes. They officially adopted the Declaration of Independence on July 4.

The defiance in John Hancock's face can be seen in this illustration that shows the moment he signed the Declaration of Independence.

This illustration from 1880 creates the scene of the first public reading of the Declaration of Independence in 1776.

The Declaration of Independence was printed in the *Pennsylvania Evening Post* on July 6. The first public reading was in Philadelphia on July 8. On August 2, 1776, the Continental Congress officially signed the Declaration of Independence.

DEMOCRACY AND THE UNITED STATES CONSTITUTION

The Declaration of Independence marked the first time that people had written a statement that claimed they had the right to choose how they were governed. This idea is known as **democracy**. The **Constitution** is the foundation of the United States' government. It expands on the democratic ideas expressed in the Declaration of Independence.

The Declaration of Independence inspired people all over the world. People in other countries organized revolutions to fight for democracy. One example is France. In 1789, the French Revolution started. The revolution was successful, and France's king was replaced by a democratic government. The 1789 French Declaration of the Rights of Man and Citizen was inspired by the ideals of the Declaration of Independence. Many other countries were also inspired to model their declarations of independence after that of the United States. This is true of Venezuela in 1811, Liberia in 1847, and Vietnam in 1945.

The illustration seen here is in the Carnavalet Museum in Paris, France. It presents the Declaration of the Rights of Man and of the Citizen. This act was passed in France on August 26, 1789.

THE MOST FAMOUS DOCUMENT OF THE UNITED STATES

Many historians have devoted their careers to studying the Declaration of Independence. Because it is such an important document for the United States, these scholars want to study different versions and revisions to understand what the writers were thinking.

What we know about the writing of the Declaration of Independence is limited by what was left behind. Our knowledge is based on newspaper articles, letters, drafts, and other writing by the people involved. These give us a picture of events, but that picture is never complete. We could still discover facts that add to our knowledge of this historical event.

There are many facts about the Declaration of Independence that many citizens do not know. Did you know, for example, that New York did not adopt the Declaration of Independence on July 4? It sat out the vote and adopted the declaration on July 15. There is much to learn. Thousands of books have been written about this most important document.

GLOSSARY

American Revolution (uh-MER-uh-ken reh-vuh-LOO-shun) Battles that soldiers from the colonies fought against Britain for freedom, from 1775 to 1783.

colonies (KAH-luh-neez) New places where people move that are still ruled by the leaders of the country from which they came.

Constitution (kon-stih-TOO-shun) The basic rules by which the United States is governed.

democracy (dih-MAH-kruh-see) A government that is run by the people who live under it.

document (DOK-yoo-ment) A written or printed statement that gives official information about something.

French and Indian War (FRENCH AND IN-dee-un WOR) The battles fought between 1754 and 1763 by England, France, and Native Americans for control of North America.

Parliament (PAR-leh-ment) The group of people in England that makes the country's laws.

protested (pro-TEST-ed) Acted out in disagreement of something.

representatives (reh-prih-ZEN-tuh-tivz) People picked to speak for others.

resolution (reh-zuh-LOO-shun) A formal statement adopted by a group of people.

taxes (TAKS-ez) Money added to the price of things or paid to a government for community services.

INDEX

PRIMARY SOURCE LIST

Page 6: *Life of George Washington—the Soldier,* created in 1854 by Régnier, Lemercier, Paris. The lithograph shows George Washington during the Battle of Monongahela on July 9, 1755, from the original painting by Junius Brutus Stearns (1810-1885).

Page 7: *The Repeal, or the Funeral of Miss Ame-Stamp,* 1766. Prints and Photographs Division, Library of Congress, Washington, D.C.

Page 9: *The Battles of Lexington and Concord, 19 April 1775,* engraving from the book *A Child's History of the United States* by John Gilmary Shea. Published in 1872 byHess and McDavitt, New York.

Page 11: *Leaders of the Continental Congress 1775: John Adams, Robert Morris, Alexander Hamilton, Thomas Jefferson,* drawing by Augustus Tholey in 1894. Stored at the Library of Congress, Washington, D.C.

Page 13: *Die Anländung der Englischen Trouppen zu Neu Yorck / Debarquement des troupes engloises a Nouvelle Yorck / The Landing of British Troops in New York, 1776,* engraving by Franz Xavier Habermann (1721–1796).

Page 16: *The United States Declaration of Independence July 4, 1776,* engraving made by printer William J. Stone in 1823. The original is exhibited in the Rotunda for the Charters of Freedom in Washington, D.C.

Page 18: *John Hancock's Defiance: July 4th 1776,* engraving made in 1876 by Currier & Ives, New York.

Page 19: *First Public Reading of the Declaration of Independence 1776,* illustration from *Harper's Weekly* in 1880, by Harper & Brothers, New York.

Page 21: *Declaration of the Rights of Man and of the Citizen* by Jean-Jacques-François Le Barbier (1738–1826) in 1789. It is housed at the Carnavalet Museum, Paris, France.

WEBSITES

Due to the changing nature of Internet links, PowerKids Press has developed an online list of websites related to the subject of this book. This site is updated regularly. Please use this link to access the list: www.powerkidslinks.com/soah/decl